THE WORLD UNMADE

The World Unmade
Frank Ormsby

A collaboration between
THE IRELAND CHAIR OF POETRY

and

UNIVERSITY COLLEGE DUBLIN PRESS
Preas Choláiste Ollscoile Bhaile Átha Cliath
2023

First published 2023
by University College Dublin Press
UCD Humanities Institute, Room H103,
Belfield,
Dublin 4

www.ucdpress.ie

ISBN 978-1-910820-79-7
ISSN 2009-8065

The Poet's Chair series is kindly supported by the Arts Council.

CIP data available from the British Library

The right of Frank Ormsby to be identified as the
author of this work has been asserted by him.

Typeset in Adobe Kepler by
Gough Typesetting Limited, Dublin
Text design by Lyn Davies Design
Printed in England on acid-free paper
by CPI Antony Rowe, Chippenham, Wiltshire.

Contents

Foreword

Probably of all the art forms, poetry appeals and puzzles the most. It is called upon in joy and grief, to commemorate a past, imagine a future, and it happens in intimate settings and on occasions of public trauma and celebration.

The Ireland Chair of Poetry has sought to reflect on this paradox since its inception in 1998 as a cross-border collaboration involving the two Arts Councils in Ireland, north and south, Queen's University Belfast, Trinity College Dublin and University College Dublin to honour Seamus Heaney's Nobel Prize for Literature in 1995.

The Trustees of the Chair in collaboration with UCD Press are delighted to follow up on previous valuable publications with the fruits of Professor Frank Ormsby's tenure, as he considers profoundly the pathways of his distinguished career. Here is the poetry of the Troubles, the impact of *The Honest Ulsterman* – the journal he edited for 20 years, which set the tone for and led the way in representations of the Troubles – and a conversation with renowned critic and editor Dr Lucy Collins of University College Dublin, touching on a range of contemporary themes, including the public role of the poet.

In his long career – he reminds us that his first published poem was in *The Honest Ulsterman* in 1969 – Frank Ormsby has worked in the private sphere, writing prize-winning collections which have gathered plaudits from around the world, most recently opening new perspectives on his Parkinson's diagnosis. But uniquely also, his editing of a series of anthologies helped define universally kinds of artistic response to crises – most dramatically civic violence in *Poets from the North of Ireland* (1979, 1990) and *A Rage for Order* (1992), but also in more personal material such as *The Long Embrace: Twentieth Century Irish Love Poems* (1987).

This is a creative artist with considerable critical power but, when he became the eighth holder of the Ireland Chair of Poetry in 2019, no one could have predicted the upheaval ushered in by the Covid 19 pandemic, which at once made his tenure difficult, unusual but also triumphant.

These pages feature a roll call of great names of contemporary poetry, some in the very heat of composing great poems. When Professor Ormsby says poetry 'elevates what is normal, preserves what is humane and teaches us to be compassionate and tolerant', it is a simple description, one which has all the hallmarks of both experience and accuracy.

I must thank Professor Ormsby and Dr Collins, and all of my fellow Trustees, both former and currently serving, ably supported by administrator Eoin Rogers, under the new stewardship of Poetry Ireland. In partnership, the Chair continues to illuminate our shared culture.

LIAM HANNAWAY
Chair of the Board of Trustees, Ireland Chair of Poetry
June 2023

The Honest Ulsterman Revisited

I am conscious that many of you in the audience were not born when *The Honest Ulsterman* made its first appearance in local bookstores and that the magazine may require a brief introduction. It was founded in 1968 and existed in print form for 111 issues, making it one of the longest running literary magazines in the British Isles. I became co-editor in 1969 and was then involved for the next 20 years, most of that time as sole editor. I should say also that this is not a comprehensive history of *The Honest Ulsterman*, it is rather an anecdotal account of the first 22 years. I have not touched on the editors who came after me – Robert Johnstone, Tom Clyde, Ruth Carr and John Wilson Foster.

The Honest Ulsterman dished out a considerable amount of harsh criticism in the period covered by this lecture and, as we shall see, the magazine itself frequently came under attack, particularly in the early years when James Simmons and Michael Foley bore the brunt. I got off lightly. Only two or three abusive letters in 20 years! I mention this because one of the letters was expressed with such vigour that I almost printed it; and still enjoy quoting it: 'Fuck you,' said the writer, 'Fuck you and your little cow-shed den of agrarian Romantics.' Otherwise, the letter was traditionally abusive, offering precise instructions as to how I should dispose of the magazine, specifying the orifice to be employed and the degree of force that should be used.

When the first issue of the magazine appeared, you had only to look at the front cover to have a sense of it as something other than the standard literary mag of the period. There was a round tower and a photo of Louis MacNeice and a list of contents which included 'Humanism', 'Hashish', and a new song. On the front cover, the magazine heralded itself as revolutionary and again on the contents page as 'a monthly handbook for revolution'. Clearly, we were not dealing with a companion to *Phoenix* or *Threshold*, the most prominent Ulster literary magazines of the period, unless the local literati had gone buck mad in the night and were plotting to overthrow the state of Northern Ireland.

The editorial, unsigned, asserted that 'Literature starts and finishes with men talking to men', and that 'the most important thing for men talking to men is to be honest'. The tone of this editorial is challenging with an undercurrent of excitement. The writer is serious, he has a vision, he means business. Having promised honesty, he goes on to explain the significance of the 'Ulsterman' half of the title:

> Just as it is necessary for each individual to claim his own freedom and make his own decisions, so it is important for the regions, small, manageable social units, to establish their own independence.

It is evident that the writer has read John Hewitt's articles on Regionalism. Indeed, some key Hewitt poems – 'From the Tibetan' and 'The Search', for example, were published in early issues of the magazine.

Who was this anonymous visionary reaching out from Gardner's and other bookshops, urging us all to embrace a revolution? He was James Simmons, a poet from Derry who had studied at the University of Leeds where his contemporaries included the poets Tony Harrison, Jon Silkin, Geoffrey Hill, Wole Soyinka, Thomas Blackburn and Brendan Kennelly. Harrison, whose versatility embraced poetry, drama and translation, may have been a particularly strong influence. The two collaborated on a translation of *Aiken Mata*, a version of Aristophanes' *Lysistrata*, published by Oxford University Press. They also lectured together for several years in Nigeria, and it was while there that Simmons witnessed a brutal civil war at close quarters – a kind of preparation perhaps for his experience of similar troubles in the north of Ireland.

Following his return to Belfast in July 1967, while he awaited publication of his first full collection, *Late but in Earnest*, by the Bodley Head, he came to feel that he was somehow on the periphery of the Ulster literary scene and his frustration grew. Luckily, he had inherited some money from his father, enough to live on for about a year, and in a memoir of the period, published in Issue 95, he recounts how 'the notion of a magazine grew on me as a way of reaching people on my own terms'. With his nephew, Michael Stephens, he set off on a reading tour of the north of England, visiting such people as Harry Chambers, Jon Silkin and Tom Pickard, each of whom was engaged in work on literary magazines dedicated to the ideal of regionalism. This would become one of the main themes of *The Honest Ulsterman*.

But beyond what Simmons calls 'these personal and political factors' he was also aware that this was a time of immense social and political upheaval:

> a time of idealistic ferment abroad, of student protest and street marching. Terence O'Neill was trying to liberalise the Northern Ireland parliament and students in Belfast and Dublin were becoming conscious of the possibility of change.

In Simmons' case these factors coalesced to produce *The Honest Ulsterman*, the aims and objectives of which were summarised in his manifesto, published in April 1968, before the first issue. In the manifesto he asserts that the magazine will aim to provide:

> an opportunity for the best Ulster writers to be read regularly in their own country [and] to contribute to the new liveliness in Ulster's cultural life.

The heart of the manifesto runs as follows:

> What is a writer but a man who feels the need to speak to strangers and make strangers glad to listen?

We will try to be independent, honest and entertaining.

In *The Honest Ulsterman* intellectual writers will be able to reach an audience outside the universities and specialist publications.

Popular and amateur writers who want to write with a little more courage and care will be welcome.

This implies no lowering of standards for a literary magazine. In fact, it asks for clarity, feeling and humour to be added to specialist qualifications and high seriousness.

We will try to rescue literature from the academics and folk art from the world of fashion and big business. In fact, we will by-pass the middle men.

Fired up by this spirit of optimism, Simmons proceeded to print two thousand copies of the first issue and to bring out an issue every month for the next seventeen months – the result was inevitable, very few copies were sold and others were returned to book stores by those who were expecting a Paisleyite publication.

I should say at this point that my involvement with *The Honest Ulsterman* was largely a matter of coincidence and good luck. In February 1969 my first 'proper' poem, so to speak, was accepted by Simmons and published in Issue 10, even though, as he pointed out, it had strong elements of 'Heaney pastiche'. Heaney, who was one of my tutors in the Department of English, praised the poem and asked me to have coffee with him in the Students' Union. He also invited me to join the writers' group that met in the Department of English every fortnight to discuss the members' work. This was hugely significant for me, but perhaps equally so was the fact that through Heaney I encountered another student who was already involved with the magazine. On the steps of the Union, Heaney was greeted by Michael Foley, a poet from Derry whose first poems had also appeared in the magazine and who already knew both Heaney and Simmons. He revealed that Simmons was feeling the strain of publishing a magazine every month and wanted Foley to take over the editorship. Foley was willing to do this, provided that the number of issues per year was reduced and that he had the help of a co-editor. I volunteered and so began my 20-year association with the magazine.

To return to the magazine itself, the issues edited by James Simmons were broad in content and featured a 'Thought for the Month' quotation which reflected Simmons' reading and helped keep alive the idea of the magazine as a vehicle for revolution. He was keen to publish some of the material he had accumulated while in Nigeria. However, perhaps aware that this might make *The Honest Ulsterman* appear to be some sort of vanity project, he chose to use a variety of pseudonyms such as Stanley Cromie and Derek Montgomery. In this way he was able to contribute long unsigned articles, editorials, poems and, reflecting his secondary career as a singer-songwriter, new songs.

Some of the poems published in the magazine at this time reveal the difficulties Simmons was experiencing as an editor. His poem, 'Censorship', published in Issue 7, describes a confrontation with the manager of 'a crappy bookshop in a country town' over the content and language of a poem by Tony Harrison:

> 'This is pure dirt,' he says. I shake my head.
> It's true, it's funny and it should be read.
> He says: 'We've got school children in the shop
> And people have complained. We'll have to stop
> Taking your magazine if you print dirt.'

In contrast, in Issue 13, a poem by a local writer, Patrick Stevenson, expresses a more literary type of hostility. Stevenson laments that 'instead of Ulster's miseries and glories' he finds 'obscene fables' and:

> a mess
> of typographical errors, wretched paper,
> transparently revealing, like still water,
> the dregs and refuse thrown into a well.
> Is this the best of Ulster? This her smell?

While Simmons' instinct was to ignore such criticism and maintain the magazine's independence, this was not always possible. In fact, Issue 11, Michael Stephens' guest issue begins with an announcement:

There should also have been three poems by John Chadbon, but intimidation on our printers by the police (just doing our job) meant that we had to cut them out.

Also missing (courtesy of Ulster's unofficial Censor) a poem by Richard Brautigan and A Thought for the Month quoted from William Burroughs.

The puritans also weighed in when the Very Reverend Doctor Alfred Martin, a former Moderator of the Presbyterian Church, and the Reverend Desmond Mock led a campaign against the magazine. Dr Martin condemned what he regarded as the depravity and indecency of the contents and urged the government to have it banned from the province, while Reverend Mock treated readers of the *Belfast Telegraph* to a similar harangue. Simmons was not cowed, and in reply attacked the Presbyterian Church and warned against censorship:

> An uncorrupted church would welcome *The Honest Ulsterman,* for the work of young writers, whose words I have the privilege of printing, has more spiritual authority, is more serious and honest than a whole wilderness of Ulster sermons.

Fortunately, Simmons had enough support from friends, journalists and contributors to help the magazine withstand the forces working against it, but by Issue 17 he was suffering from editorial fatigue and a certain disappointment that most of the poems submitted were what he called 'personal, lyrical, fragmentary' rather than work that engaged seriously with public issues. He decided to step down and Michael Foley and I became joint editors.

Foley had been a kind of editor-in-waiting after his guest editorship of Issue 13 and, as a passionate polemicist, he wanted to turn the magazine into a more iconoclastic and rumbustious publication. Rather ironically, our first joint decision was to scrap the subtitle, 'monthly handbook for a revolution', because, if I recall accurately, we found it embarrassing and naive and open to ridicule.

Foley then fixed his attention on the literary scene in Belfast, which he regarded as having elevated Seamus Heaney, Derek Mahon and Michael Longley over James Simmons. He nicknamed these three the 'tight-assed trio' and set about his targets with a verve that was scathing and sometimes vitriolic. Seeking to define what makes a good writer, he seems to embrace Patrick Kavanagh's championing of sweeping statement as the only opinion worth listening to. He is attracted to Kavanagh's comment that having the courage of one's own opinions is best – even when the opinions are unacceptable. He also emphasises the importance of a sense of the absurd. The writer will also be aware of his own defects and, like the laughing fishmonger, put his arse in the window for a cod.

Foley's voice is at its most recognisable in Issue 24 to which he contributes a satirical blast in rhyming couplets, entitled 'The Poet's Circus'. The chief target is the writers' group at Queen's, which is castigated as phoney and content to fondle rather than strike. The poem builds up to a rejection of what he regards as authorial back scratching:

> Enough of poets! I have plans
> For boozy nights with soccer fans...
> I won't be read or talked about
> Or photographed with pints of stout
> Or sealed off (AAGH! the mummy's curse!)
> In Penguin Books of Irish Verse

As noted, Foley was strongly of the opinion that the critical elevation of Heaney and Mahon downgraded Simmons, who he regarded as a poet willing to take risks while the others played safe. He accused them of having lost their innovative qualities and become part of the 'Establishment'. However, pressed by Simmons among others to abandon his campaign, Foley gave in to the pressure. At this stage, the magazine was in danger of folding, but staged a sturdy revival, prompted perhaps by the quality of some of the contributions at this time, as well as the impetus that had grown steadily over the course of 30 issues.

It was not long after this that Michael Foley decided to relocate to London and I became sole editor. However, *The Honest*

Ulsterman continued to struggle and I still remember the burial mound of unsold magazines that I carried with me from one flat to the next, getting larger by the year and heavier by the decade. That's not to say that the role of editor was one of unmitigated drudgery. I knew many of the main contributors personally and was editorially blessed to have a core of talented and generous writers and friends to call upon. On my way home from the Royal Belfast Academical Institution, where I worked throughout my editorship, I would call at the Eglantine Inn. By four or five o'clock, Ciaran and Deirdre Carson, John Morrow, and sometimes Michael Longley would arrive from the Arts Council, Paul Muldoon from the BBC and Ted Hickey from the Ulster Museum, where he was Keeper of Art. Books were discussed and new poems occasionally unveiled. By the time I left, I usually had contributions for the next issue of the magazine.

The magazine was often satirical in tone but rarely engaged in direct satire. Three notable exceptions were 'Man of the People: The Parliamentary Speeches of John McQuade' by Colum O'Figgis, and my own parodies, 'The Write-an-Ulster-Play Kit' and 'Tragic Anguish'. McQuade was the Unionist MP for Woodvale, a former street fighter and a notorious sectarian bigot connected to at least one Loyalist paramilitary group. Colum O'Figgis was a pseudonym for a lecturer in Law at Queen's named Harry Calvert, someone well able to tread a delicate line between the libellous and non-libellous. The focus of 'Man of the People' is McQuade's 'remarkable' speech in the House of Commons chamber of the Parliament of Northern Ireland, 16 October 1968. O'Figgis declares his desire to alert a wider audience to this 'magnificent address' but his true intentions may be gauged from the following introduction:

> Perhaps once in several decades, the British parliamentary system throws up a remarkable rhetorical giant, whose oratorical genius uniquely expresses the mood of the time. It is six decades since Lloyd George appeared, and three since Winston Churchill's colossal presence first bestrode the political scene. Ours has now thrown up – and John McQuade has arrived.

The writer goes on to draw parallels with another 'John McQuade' – John Charles McQuaid, the Catholic Archbishop of Dublin, also a notorious reactionary. Given McQuade, the MP's, sectarianism, this comparison is particularly provocative. O'Figgis comments:

> So far as is known, the two men are not related. Yet both have willingly shouldered the burden, spurned by lesser men, of protecting the faith; of standing fast in the face of the Devil's hordes, whether in the guise of contraceptive pills or conspiring papists; of resisting the evil of change and buttressing the virtues of kindness, tolerance, brotherly love and equality as illuminated through Ireland's history. It is not clear that either is Christian; yet both are profoundly religious.

O'Figgis notes that, 'In a parliamentary career spanning three years' McQuade has contributed exactly 'three minor speeches... an entire parliamentary question... [and] half a dozen interjections' which he calculates add up to 'no less than 2000 words of distilled wisdom... cheap surely, [at a price to the exchequer] of £2 each.' He then quotes each in full, allowing the MP to damn himself. For example, he provides: 'the full text of [his] historic and powerful speech on the second reading of the Human Rights Bill... "Wrong! Wrong!"'

McQuade's remarks on capital punishment, discrimination, financial policy, state security and the Derry riot follow – reactionary ramblings which expose the speaker more comprehensively than he is aware.

The McQuade booklet, given free with the magazine, had a memorable aftermath. When the unionist party lawyers were unable to find grounds to sue, McQuade, the old street fighter, came to the fore. He arrived at the premises of the printer, Regency Press, removed his jacket and threatened to settle the matter himself. To the credit of Regency Press, they refused to be bullied.

This satire on McQuade never raises its voice. In contrast, the 'Write-an-Ulster-Play-Kit' editorial and the 'Tragic Anguish' piece employ a kind of ridicule. The play kit is an alphabetical guide to the key aspects of a typical Ulster play and it is offered as a comic summary of the form: its enslavement to stereotypes, predictable plots and platitudinous ideas. A couple of examples will illustrate the prevalent tone. Firstly, the prospective playwright will find it essential to mention such humorous paradoxes as the fact that:

> William of Orange fought *with the Pope's approval* at the Battle of the Boyne. Result: eye-popping consternation on the part of the lovable orange bigot.

The guide also declares that:

> a mixed marriage is indispensable. Who ever heard of an Ulster play without a mixed marriage? The marriage must lead to a crisis of allegiance in husband and/or wife; the crippling polarities of Ulster society reflected in domestic microcosm.

This feature, printed as an editorial, attracted the interest of the BBC and was broadcast on Radio Ulster. It had approving responses within the literary community. Stewart Parker, for example, who was at odds with local theatres over the rejection of his quirky, original plays, was delighted by the satire.

So, despite the uncertainties of the early 70s, the magazine survived and it was not long before the iconoclastic note echoed again over literary Belfast. Like Simmons and Foley, I took the view that to write poetry about the Troubles was to fiddle while Belfast and Derry burned and our main target was Padraic Fiacc. It was the appearance of Fiacc's Troubles anthology, *The Wearing of the Black*, that prompted a fierce critical debate on the role of poetry and the Troubles. Edna Longley had previously described Fiacc as 'Banquo at the feast' and Michael Longley had described his poems as '[buzzing] around the Ulster tragedy like a dazed bluebottle around an open wound.' My own contribution (in the double issue 46/47) was 'Tragic Anguish', a parody of a short play, in which the central character is a poet and anthologist meeting with a young disciple to discuss his poems. The older man applauds 'the aesthetic of confrontation' and commends the disciple's 'insight... despair... [and] overwhelming sense of history', adding: 'It's the same tortured anguish that compelled you to write FUCK IT ALL on that lavatory wall in downtown Belfast. The same cry from the heart.'

Fiacc was understandably angry about these attacks on his anthology. The feeling among the book's critics was that many of the poems were self-indulgent and lacked literary merit, but Fiacc saw these opinions as personal attacks on himself as a poet and anthologist. John Hewitt tactfully suggested that I give Fiacc some space to answer his critics and the result was a tirade in Issue 50. Fiacc began with a kind of rampage against what he called the 'Earnest Honest Ulster Establishment of pee-the-bed Pyjama Poets', declaring:

> I know three Faber poets personally and they have in common an 'odour of sanctity'. Talking to any one of them is always like talking to a holy picture. They answer back like old-time students for the priesthood and the wee-est one of them all talks down his nose to you like a Bishop. Why is this? The answer is because getting published by Faber is canonisation in one's own lifetime. It means: 'Who's like me since Leather Arse died?'

He continues:

> The bad odour surrounding *The Wearing of the Black* is the odour of blood and it stinks of a society that has hopelessly degraded itself and consequently degraded those of us who have to exist in it. *The Wearing of the Black* is a mass of unpalatable truths that I have used or misused poetry to confront.

He goes on to castigate those Ulster poets who seem untouched by the violence all around them, particularly if such a poet is: 'insulated in some university shelter belt or other, or is ensconced in some cultural oasis such as the Arts Council or the BBC.'

However, writers who were perceived to be exploiting the Troubles came under attack again in Issue 53 of the magazine when the following advertisement appeared:

For Hire
Qualified War Poet
- Prepared to bleed in public;
- Documentary realism guaranteed – legs, arms, bits in polythene bags etc. provided;
- Was in Northern Ireland on Bloody Sunday, Bloody Monday, Bloody Tuesday, Bloody Wednesday, Bloody Thursday, Bloody Friday, Bloody Saturday;
- Would like to meet genuine publisher/producer with a view to furthering career.

The intense focus on acceptable and unacceptable ways of writing about the Troubles became a kind of crusade in *The Honest Ulsterman* and other magazines. Some of the leading poets made authoritative statements that provoked much discussion and debate within the literary community. Seamus Heaney remarked that, for Northern Irish poets, poetry 'moved from being simply a matter of achieving the satisfactory verbal icon to being a search for images and symbols adequate to our predicament.' Michael Longley commented that a poet 'would be inhuman if he did not respond to tragic events in his own community and a poor artist if he did not seek to endorse that response imaginatively.' But he also stated his conviction that 'the artist needs time in which to allow the raw material of experience to settle to an imaginative depth.' These statements were published elsewhere but reflected the concerns of the magazine and as the editor I was determined not to publish poems or prose which responded simplistically to the latest atrocity. I came in for criticism when the magazine failed to react to the events of Bloody Sunday. Rightly or wrongly, it seemed appropriate at the time to avoid the self-importance and inadequacy of responses on such occasions. Now, nearly 50 years later, I regret that silence and appreciate that every extra voice would have given the multitude of protests and condemnations additional weight.

The poetry reviews in *The Honest Ulsterman* were a significant element in the voice of the magazine. Outstanding critics such as Edna Longley and Michael Allen wrote outstanding criticism of the Seamus Heaney, Michael Longley, Derek Mahon, James

Simmons generation and of the poets who followed – such as Paul Muldoon, Medbh McGuckian and Ciaran Carson. The review section was often abrasive, contentious, impertinent. At times it resembled a series of skirmishes – Fiacc, Simmons, Foley versus everyone; Ormsby versus Hewitt; Carson versus Heaney; Heaney versus Foley.

Carson's review of Seamus Heaney's *North* in Issue 50 emerged from a mildly heated argument at which I was present during the launch of *North* in the Ulster Museum. Heaney, stung perhaps by some of Carson's observations, suggested that I should get Carson to review the collection for *The Honest Ulsterman*. I grasped the opportunity and the review, titled 'Escaped from the Massacre?' has been sparking interest among critics ever since. Carson speculates that Heaney:

> seems to have moved – unwillingly, perhaps – from being a writer with the gift of precision, to become the laureate of violence – a mythmaker, an anthropologist of ritual killing, an apologist for 'the situation', in the last resort, a mystifier.

While acknowledging the precision of what he regards as the best poems in *North*, Carson regrets how other poems:

> degenerate into a messy historical and religious surmise – a kind of Golden Bough activity, in which the real difference between our society and that of Jutland in some vague past are glossed over for the sake of the parallels of ritual.

The review ends with the stinging observation: 'Everyone was anxious that *North* should be a great book; when it turned out that it wasn't, it was treated as one anyway.' I had a similar run-in with John Hewitt in 1971 when I reviewed his pamphlet collection, *An Ulster Reckoning*, issued with a foreword in which Hewitt quotes John Montague's description of him as: 'the first (and the last) deliberately Ulster Protestant poet. That designation carries a heavy obligation these days.' In the court of *The Honest Ulsterman*, this counted as posturing. Hewitt sent a review copy of the pamphlet to the magazine with a note to the effect that he expected 'the usual dismissive mention'. I commented that it was not difficult to give second-rate poetry a spurious importance by playing this game – let's call it 'The Dilemma of the Ulster Protestant Poet' or, 'Look I've Got a Split Identity'. Hewitt wrote to me from Coventry where he was curator of the Herbert Art Gallery, suggesting that I could develop a more effective 'hatchet-man' style by imitating models such as William Hazlitt. Moved by the dignified anger in the letter, I wrote an apology and it was accepted. I met Hewitt the following year when he retired from the gallery and he and his wife, Roberta, returned to Belfast. He became a benign, generous presence, offering advice in a most sensitive and unobtrusive way.

The poems in *The Honest Ulsterman* gave the magazine its unique voice but there were prose writers also who were an important part of the chorus. Some of Bernard MacLaverty's early stories for example, are to be found in *The Honest Ulsterman* and it is impossible to think of the magazine without the contribution of the pseudonymous writers, 'Jude the Obscure' whose 'Business Section' appeared consistently from the early 70s, and the dark Rabelaisian humour of what John Morrow called his 'pieces'. 'Jude the Obscure' made his first pseudonymous appearance in the November/December 1970 issue, number 26, as Joe Biggar, author of 'A cautious experiment: A tale for married men'. It was accompanied by a letter to the editors which declared:

> I am a little old to intrude myself on your happy-little-mag-high-jinks: which is to say I work at a very ordinary job, love one wife, drink almost not at all and spend a lot of time helping my son with his homework. However, I abhor Sunday writers, am not one, and believe that good writing is a derivative of ordinary living – like sweat.

He concluded that the twentieth century would 'have to grow up some day and have the guts to throw away 90% of the rubbish swallowed as art in its adolescence'. In a moment of epiphany, Michael Foley recognised that here was someone who might make a formidable columnist. The outcome was '*The Honest Ulsterman* Business Section', which made its debut in the July/August 1971 issue, number 29, under the penname 'Jude the Obscure'. Jude spent the next three decades exciting and irritating its readers, skirmishing with the Dublin literati, particularly with John Jordan in the pages of *Hibernia,* and releasing extracts from his novel *First Chronicle of Farset.*

Speculation over the years, that 'Jude the Obscure' was James Simmons or me, were well clear of the mark. 'Jude' was a Belfast man in his early 50s named Gerry Keenan, who worked in the cabinet office in London. He had a patchy literary background in that he had contributed to such publications as *The Bell, Lagan* and *Kavanagh's Weekly,* and the self-educated man's passionate relationship with literature, poetry, and music. His conversation was preachy and dictatorial, opinionated, and often patronising. As I speak, I can see him take on an emphatic tone. He is telling me off for not using my vote or admiring the poetry of W. R. Rodgers or John Montague. Or he is speaking in praise of Kavanagh. I imagine that he carried the aura of Belfast intellectuals like those who frequented Davey McLean's Progressive Bookshop. The range of subjects in the 'Business Section' was remarkable: one of 'Jude's' mottos was that 'Excellence must be recognised when it occurs' and he found this excellence in many places – in the work of the illustrator George Ade, the novels of Henry Green and J. F. Powers, the paintings of Edward Hopper, John Sloan and Winslow Homer. There were severe maulings, however, for C. S. Lewis, Henri De Montherland and Edward Wilson.

'Jude' was a mischievous middle-class Catholic, almost chaste in his writing. Not so John Morrow, the other pillar of *Honest Ulsterman* prose. Morrow (real name John Windrim) was a working-class Protestant from East Belfast and the 'pieces' he wrote reflected his own experiences and became what might be called the texture of the magazine. He described himself as 'Blackmouth' and summarised his career as:

> Public Elementary, shipyard at fourteen, linen trade at sixteen, with some success as a singer during the folk revival, now a late developed delinquent masquerading as a solid suburbanite.

Morrow was large and voluble like his characters and had a rich fund of black humorous stories. His speciality was bawdy black humour and had he begun contributing to the early issues of the magazine, the censor would have had a busy time. Morrow's 'pieces' are peopled by the larger than life. I think, for example, of the boxer with a bad heart in 'A Heart and a Half':

> Jack Lynch from Lurgan was the name he fought under. Held the heavyweight Championship of Mrs Copley's Circus in the Chapel Fields for two weeks. Great days them were; thirty bob a fight, win or lose – ten for him, ten for his Da an' ten for me. The Da managed him and I carried the bucket.

And in 'What a Pixture' there is Sammy:

> a tight wee man in the physical traditions of Cagney and Edward G., those dwarf gangsters beloved by a previous generation in a city where big men were either bog-reared peelers, bailiffs or Means Test snoopers from the 'Brew'.

His characters are absurd men of action:

> 'Kipper-hips' the Olympic walker. Six-foot tall like a yard of pump water. Roun' and roun' the sea docks in his simmit and drawers with Joker on the stop-watch. The arse goin' like two eggs in a hankie. Finished up with dropped arches an' a slipped disk.

The Honest Ulsterman was, first and foremost, a poetry magazine which also happened to publish short stories, extracts from novels and much else. Simmons' generation contributed eagerly, as indeed did John Hewitt, and other poets of the 1940s, such as Roy McFadden and Robert Greacen, were re-activated so to speak, at least partly by the energies of *The Honest Ulsterman*. It was also clear that Simmons' manifesto was in part filtered through Hewitt's key texts about Regionalism. Meanwhile, the younger poets such as Ciaran Carson, Paul Muldoon and Michael Foley were establishing themselves. In other words, the magazine reflected a continuity that was about to become a characteristic of Ulster poetry, never before so strongly evident. It was also evident that Simmons would maintain his links with English poets such as Tony Harrison, Stevie Smith and Roger McGough. Several of these poets became part of what might be called the 'voice' of *The Honest Ulsterman*. I am thinking, in particular, of Gavin Ewart and Carol Rumens. Witty, inventive, bawdy, technically skilful, Ewart might have been born to grace the pages of *The Honest Ulsterman* and he was a contributor throughout the magazine's existence.

Worth remembering also was the part played by the magazine in the re-emergence of Carol Rumens. She had published a book entitled *A Strange Girl in Bright Colours* (1973), but it was when she had a dozen poems accepted for the magazine and had a pamphlet, *A Necklace of Mirrors*, issued by Ulsterman publications that she really took wing. Indeed, Ulsterman publications, the pamphlet series associated with the magazine, is itself worth more attention than I can give it here. Over 40 pamphlets were published and they included the first and earliest collections of practically every Ulster poet who went on to establish a reputation. These poets' voices gave *The Honest Ulsterman* its own unique sound.

As for the impact and influence of the magazine, that is probably best assessed by a neutral reader. I can give only a subjective sense of why a poetry magazine, published in Belfast, with only a tiny circulation (about 400 copies per issue) seemed to matter, if it can be said to matter. Firstly, it was an invaluable outlet for emerging poets and writers already established. It survived robustly for over 20 years in the world of the literary magazine where publications spring up and disappear overnight. Secondly, the fact that the magazine's life coincided with the Northern Ireland Troubles, gave it the significance that all creative work has in time of conflict. It preserved peace time values and kept them warm, as it were, during the most destructive phases and acted as a foundation for the aftermath of the Troubles.

As already shown in this lecture, another preoccupation of the magazine's regular contributors was the role of the artist in times of upheaval, and whether the Troubles should be approached directly or obliquely. These matters gave a focus and intensity that attracted a considerable amount of critical attention among reviewers and academics. The poetry in the magazine was varied and wide ranging. The poems of James Simmons, in particular, dealt with marriage, infidelity and divorce and there was a suburban dimension in the poems of Gavin Ewart, W. Price Turner and many others – none of them 'agrarian romantics', by the way. In fact, the poetry of *The Honest Ulsterman* would, in itself, merit a full-scale study, as would the manner in which it cleared the way for key anthologies such as *Poets from the North of Ireland* and *A Rage for Order: Poetry of the Northern Ireland Troubles*. It may also have led to the re-emergence of a neglected older-generation poet, George Buchanan, who featured prominently in Issue 59. There were issues dedicated to The Belfast Group, World War II in the North of Ireland, Louis MacNeice, the 'Folk' poetry of W. F. Marshall and – as I have already mentioned in passing – the series of poetry pamphlets issued by Ulsterman Publications.

Next, an observation. *The Honest Ulsterman* writers also deserve a fresh lease. A strong case could be made for resurrecting John Morrow's 'pieces' and his two novels, *The Confessions of Proinsias O'Toole* and *The Essex Factor*. In particular, it is time to reissue the poems of James Simmons. The poet who wrote 'Stephano Remembers' and 'Didn't He Ramble' to name but two, deserves a new 'Selected'.

I began with an irascible letter to me and my 'little cow-shed den of agrarian romantics'. I'd like to round off with another letter to an editor. The editor in this case is Michael Foley and the writer Seamus Heaney. Heaney's verse-letter is sometimes sardonic, sometimes good-humoured, a riposte to the critical barrage against the poets of the Group. The approach is playful but with a serious undercurrent, rather like that of the magazine itself:

Letter to an Editor

Michael, you know I'm expert with the spade
and get official backing for each action;
then stand back, for this folk-museum blade
can choose to lop off handshake or erection.

I warn you, your wee fly bedsitter-king
sweats in the palm of this Rachmann of the arts
who comes with fake concern and a Claddagh ring
to evict him from the reek of his own farts.

(God but his H.U. stuff, so sweet and sour
is easy going as the turnip-snedder –
I'd say at least twelve quatrains to the hour,
including tea-breaks, which gives us a newsletter,
eight times a day, going at minimum rate.
There's a vocation lost, but what's the use?
I should have read, I realise too late,
not 'The Great Hunger' but 'Collected Pruse'.)

Now didn't you learn it all from Kavanagh,
the slapdash truth and well-meaning lie?
Distrust your solemn man. Go for the ba.
And ironically don't care – spit in their eye.
Your prose style, I must say, is excellent,
fit instrument for cheek-slash and death-blow
but is all that courage at the sticking point
screwed up by the real thing or some dildo?
Official gadflies are co-opted. Then beware.
You too might lunge and find your angry stick
is dunlopillo. Who do you think you are?
Rare Ben Jonson? Swift? Dryden? Or Ulick?

We both know the Big Study and Pre Par,
the half-day syndrome and the day-boy lunch.
It would be a pity to spoil things as they are
with a clip on the ear or rabbit punch,

so instead I write to say I am fed up
finding myself too much in gossip columns.
Show proper respect, you editorial dope.
You're dealing with a prefect from St. Columb's.

Based on a lecture given at Queen's University Belfast on 13 May 2021.

The Poetry of the Troubles

It is generally true that the course of Ulster poetry since the mid-60s has been dictated by the Troubles. Well before 1968, however, the poets Louis MacNeice, John Hewitt and John Montague had already, to a greater or lesser extent, portrayed Ulster as a divided society, riven by sectarianism. Their themes and images, dating back to the 1930s, were shared by the emerging poets of the late 60s/early 70s, most notably Seamus Heaney, Michael Longley, Derek Mahon and James Simmons. By the time I produced my anthology *A Rage for Order* in 1992, poets such as Ciaran Carson, Paul Muldoon and Tom Paulin had also begun to contribute significantly to the poetry of the Troubles. Since that time, even post-ceasefire, these poets have continued to produce work that reflects the aftermath of violence, the legacy of trauma and the struggle for normality, alongside a new generation of voices such as Sinéad Morrissey, Leontia Flynn, Alan Gillis and Colette Bryce.

In this lecture I intend to revisit the poetry of *A Rage for Order* before considering the wealth of new material published since 1992. As early as 1934, MacNeice's poem 'Valediction', published in *Poems* (1935), portrays Belfast as 'Built on reclaimed mud', a symbol of a society with insecure foundations. It is the result, he implies, of the tension between the warring factions of the North: the 'devout and profane and hard' Ulster and the seductive spirit of Ireland which is, nevertheless, inbred and violent. Section 16 of MacNeice's book-length *Autumn Journal*, begun in 1938 and published the following year, is an extended reflection on Ireland in general and the North in particular. The themes and images of this section make it a source text for the Troubles poetry written after 1968 as it refers to the sectarian tension, intransigence and violence of earlier troubles in the York Street area of Belfast during MacNeice's boyhood. Among its themes are the complex, turbulent relationship between Ireland and Britain, the Irishman's love/hate engagement with his country (also a prominent theme in 'Valediction') and the artist's envy of the man of action. We are shown a society where 'free speech is nipped in the bud' and the 'minority is always guilty'. The predominant imagery is of drums, bombs, banners, and sectarian graffiti, and of Belfast, again as a city 'built upon mud'.

Twenty-five years after the appearance of MacNeice's *Collected Poems* in 1966, John Hewitt's *Collected Poems* (1991) brought into focus the work of a poet who had, for decades, explored the dilemma of those who, like himself, were descended from the English and Scottish settlers who had colonised Ulster in the early seventeenth century. As an assistant in the Belfast Museum and Art Gallery from November 1930, Hewitt began to engage profoundly with the local, historical past, developing a life-long admiration for the radical, liberal Presbyterians who flourished in the late eighteenth century. In poems such as 'Once Alien Here' from *No Rebel Word* (1948), and 'The Colony' from *Collected Poems 1932–1967* (1968), Hewitt negotiates the crosscurrents in which the liberal Ulsterman of Planter stock finds himself caught. The speaker in these poems is sufficiently rooted in the Province to feel 'native' in his 'thought', and insists his ancestors have, by hard work, established shared ownership. However, he is also aware of the dispossessed natives' 'savage history of wrong' ('The Glens', *Selected John Hewitt*, 1981) and tentatively desires to make amends, whilst conscious that the conciliatory impulse may not be entirely adequate. He is sensitive to the older, indigenous tradition, though suspicious of its predominant Catholicism, and yearns to achieve an individuality that draws on, and expresses, both traditions.

This is not to say that at times Hewitt is not irritated by the attitudes displayed on both sides of the social and political divide. For example, in 'The Dilemma' from *An Ulster Reckoning* (1971), Ireland is portrayed as a 'maimed', 'creed-infected' and 'ruptured' island and the poet is prompted to re-assert his rights as a descendant of the Planters; whereas, in 'The Coasters', from the same volume, he castigates the complacency and superficial liberalism of the bourgeoisie who 'coasted along' while 'the sores suppurated and spread'. A number of other Hewitt poems written after 1968 should also be mentioned, most notably 'Neither an Elegy nor a Manifesto' (*Out of My Time*, 1974), urging us to 'Bear in mind' the victims and casualties of violence, and the 'Postscript 1984' (*Freehold and Other Poems*, 1986), to an earlier poem, 'Ulster Names', which brands place-names now associated with atrocities as locations on a 'tarnished map... not to be read as pastoral again'.

Since the 1950s, John Montague also made the unhappy history of Ireland a central theme in his poetry. In a preface to his ambitious, book-length sequence, *The Rough Field* (1972), he recalls how, on a bus journey from Belfast to Tyrone in the early 60s, he had 'a kind of vision, in the medieval sense, of [his] home area, the unhappiness of its historical destiny', which proved to be the genesis of the poem. It is, then, partly a lament for the decline of the Gaelic tradition, partly a record of sectarianism and oppression, and partly a celebration of survival and adaptation. Montague's awareness of the 'pattern history weaves / From one small backward place' ('The Source', *The Rough Field*), informs a series of elegiac portraits of his rural Catholic ancestry whose history of dispossession and dispersal parallels in the present the destiny of the Gaelic chieftains who sailed into exile in 1607. The lyrics 'A Lost Tradition' and 'A Grafted Tongue' record the psychic damage done when a whole tradition is supplanted and reduced to 'shards'. The landscape is imagined as a manuscript that the descendent Irish have 'lost the skill to read' and the experience of having to 'grow a second tongue' as a traumatic humiliation. The penultimate section of *The Rough Field*, titled 'A New Siege', focuses once more on historical patterns, this time the parallel between the Protestant Siege of Derry in 1690 and the siege of the Catholic Bogside area in 1969. The cumulative power of *The Rough Field* is complemented by other Troubles lyrics. In 'Falls Funeral' (*A Slow Dance*, 1975), for example, the victims are the Catholic children following a child's coffin, who become for Montague:

a sight beyond tears
beyond pious belief
David's brethren
in the land of Goliath.

The young Catholics in 'Foreign Field' are victims in a different way; while the Republican sympathiser in the poem shows unexpected gallantry towards the wounded British soldier in his garden, the children who come out to play have been hardened by the violence that surrounds them and chant: 'Die, you bastard'.

By 1969 a new generation of poets had begun to respond to the developing Troubles in the North and to explore the aesthetic responsibility of the poet. For example, the poet and critic Seamus Deane, referring to the poems of Seamus Heaney and Derek Mahon, argues that in their efforts to:

> come to grips with destructive energies, they attempt to demonstrate a way of turning them towards creativity... Their sponsorship is not simply for the sake of art, it is for the energies embodied in art which have been diminished or destroyed elsewhere.

Heaney also contributed to the critical debate. In his poem 'Exposure', from *North* (1975), for example, he portrays himself as 'weighing his responsible *tristia*', and later, reflecting on the artistic dilemma facing the Ulster poet at that time, comments:

> The problem of poetry moved from being simply a matter of achieving the satisfactory verbal icon, to being a search for images and symbols adequate to our predicament.

Michael Longley clarifies just how precarious the position of the poet was when he recalls that, during the early years of the Troubles, some critics brought misguided pressure to bear on Ulster poets, pressure not unlike the chorus of 'where are the war poets?' to be heard in Britain in 1939 in response to World War II. While asserting that: 'a poet would be inhuman if he did not respond to tragic events in his own community and a poor artist if he did not seek to endorse that response imaginatively', he recalls that if the poets failed to produce recognisable Troubles poems, they were accused of evasion, of failing to fulfil their poetic responsibilities, and if they did make the Troubles a central theme, they were accused in some quarters of exploitation, rushing to produce the poetry of the latest atrocity (to adapt Conor Cruise O'Brien's phrase about instant politics). In fact, far from 'rushing' to respond to events, most Northern poets shared Longley's opinion that 'the artist needs time in which to allow the raw material of experience to settle to an imaginative depth' and therefore took the tentative, responsible way, while recognising its limitations.

Heaney may be said to have taken the creative lead. In his second collection, *Door into the Dark* (1969), he began his own quest for adequate images and symbols. In the ambiguously titled 'The Other Side', he writes from personal experience of sectarian division and evokes a delicate but powerful impulse towards reconciliation; the possibility that the speaker and his Protestant neighbour might (or might not) find common ground:

> Should I slip away, I wonder, or go up and touch his shoulder
> and ask about the weather or the price of grass-seed.

In the same collection, 'The Tolland Man' draws on Heaney's reading of P. V. Glob's *The Bog People* (1969) about the sacrificial victims of Iron Age fertility rites in Scandinavia, to suggest imaginative parallels between that society's territory-based religion and aspects of Republican mythology and iconography in contemporary Ireland. This poem pre-figures the two-section structure of Heaney's book, *North,* which attracted widespread critical attention, both positive and negative, as a Troubles collection. Broadly speaking, the opening section employs the mythic approach of 'The Tolland Man' with particular focus on the bog people. 'Punishment', for example, progresses from a portrait of an Iron Age adulteress, executed, and buried in bogland for having offended against the mores of her tribe, to the tarring and feathering of Catholic girls in Derry for fraternising with British soldiers. Through this poem Heaney confronts his own ambivalence in relation to such punishments, describing himself as an 'artful voyeur', sensitive to what is happening at the centre but maintaining an almost cagey perspective from the periphery. He confesses to a tension in himself between an urge to join in the chorus of 'civilised outrage' and an understanding of 'the exact / and tribal, intimate revenge'.

Elsewhere in the collection he posits the potentially assuaging power of ritual. For example, in 'Funeral Rites' he describes how:

> Now as news comes in
> of each neighbourly murder
> we pine for ceremony,
> customary rhythms:
> the temperate footsteps
> of a cortege, winding past
> each blinded home.

The second section of *North* culminates in the sequence 'Singing School', an autobiographical account of growing up in Northern Ireland – 'Fostered alike by beauty and by fear', as the epigraph from Wordsworth has it. Heaney chronicles with wry humour his beginnings as a poet in a state where he was one of a beleaguered Catholic minority. In this section, too, the challenges and difficulties of reading and writing about the Troubles are to the fore – first in 'Whatever You Say, Say Nothing' – an irritated blast against both the formulaic language of politicians and journalists and the 'famous / Northern reticence', including his own. This passionate, formidable, wide-ranging collection ends with the anxious intensity of 'Exposure', in which Heaney, now an 'émigré' living in Co. Wicklow, ponders his responsibilities as a poet, vulnerably unsure of the roads he has and has not taken.

In Michael Longley's first collection, *No Continuing City* (1969), the poem 'In Memoriam' signals that one of Longley's richest sources of inspiration will be the Great War, experienced on a personal and immediate level through the anecdotes of his soldier father, who had 'looked death and nightmare in the face' at the Battle of the Somme, then imaginatively, through the poetry and prose of soldier poets such as Wilfred Owen and Edward

Thomas. However, after 1969, his poems of the First and Second World Wars took on an additional dimension and, as the title of his second collection, *An Exploded View* (1973), indicates, his response to the 'tragic events in the community' became as much a preoccupation for him as they were for Heaney. He is not as obsessively concerned with Irish history as Heaney and Montague, but he displays an awareness of the cultural divisions in Ireland that have fractured communities and affirms the importance of poetry as one of the reservoirs of positive, civilised values in times of chaos.

One of the most compelling examples is 'Wounds'. Here his father's memories of the Ulster Division at the Somme – its courage, its prejudices, its teenage dead – and the fact that his father's death many years after the war was partly a result of his war wounds, developed into an elegy for specific victims of the Troubles. These include three young Scottish soldiers lured to their death, a child killed in its nursery by a ricochet bullet and the bus conductor shot at home:

> By a shivering boy who wandered in
> Before they could turn the television down
> Or tidy away the supper dishes.

Indeed, the focus in Longley's Troubles poems, is constantly on the victims and, in particular, on the destruction of domestic and familiar securities. In the sequence titled 'Wreaths' (*The Echo Gate*, 1979), a civil servant is preparing an Ulster fry for breakfast when he is wounded in his kitchen, a greengrocer is shot serving behind his counter and ten linen workers, slaughtered on their way home from work, are portrayed as dying among their scattered wallets, spectacles, and dentures.

The complex inter-weaving of themes and images in Longley's work is evident in the way his nature poems, especially those set in the West of Ireland, often embody a consoling alternative to the conflict in the North. In 'The Ice-Cream Man', from *Gorse Fires* (1991), for example, a poem about lost innocence, Longley addresses his youngest daughter and recalls:

Rum and raisin, vanilla, butter-scotch, walnut, peach:
You would rhyme off the flavours. That was before
They murdered the ice-cream man on the Lisburn Road
And you bought carnations to lay outside his shop.

He then creates for her, a litany of 'all the wild flowers of the Burren' that he has seen on a single day to set against the brutal killing. The natural abundance celebrated here echoes that of the earlier 'Peace', translated from the Latin poet, Tibullus, in which the speaker, a reluctant soldier, sings the praises of wine, friendship, conversation, love, sex, family and old age and concludes:

As for me, I want a woman
To come and fondle my ears of wheat and let apples
Overflow between her breasts. I shall call her Peace.

As seen here, another vital strand in Longley's work derives from his grounding in Greek and Roman poetry. For example, some of his most powerful Troubles poems are filtered with consummate artistry through details from Homer, so that they are simultaneously immediate and oblique. In 'The Butchers' (*Gorse Fires*), Longley describes without comment Odysseus' vengeful slaughter of Penelope's suitors and the 'disloyal housemaids' in a way that creates disturbing echoes of the Shankill Butchers, a gang of sectarian murderers who operated in Belfast from 1975 until 1982. When the poem 'Ceasefire', from *The Ghost Orchid* (1995), appeared in the *Irish Times* in August 1994, it could be said to have been one of the first post-Troubles poems. However, as Longley later revealed:

Because at that time we were praying for an IRA ceasefire, I called the poem 'Ceasefire' and, hoping to make my own minute contribution, sent it to the *Irish Times*. It was the poem's good luck to be published two days after the IRA's declaration.

The sonnet had an enormous impact when it first appeared as it captured the chilling dilemma faced by victims' families following the ceasefire. In the poem, Priam forgives Achilles for killing his son, Hector, and says:

> 'I get down on my knees and do what must be done
> And kiss Achilles' hand, the killer of my son.'

This raises the question of whether we 'must' forgive the sins of the past in order to move towards a better future.

Like virtually all of his contemporaries, Derek Mahon calls into question the relevance and effectiveness of art in violent times. The title poem in *The Snow Party* (1975), which has a Japanese setting, juxtaposes the formal domesticities and aesthetic rituals of tea-drinking and snow-viewing in Nagoya with the bloody realities elsewhere in 'the boiling squares'. The fact that each verse of the poem is a loose variation on the haiku form reinforces our sense of the tea-drinkers as a rather decadent literary gathering. The reader is left to decide whether the 'silence / In the houses of Nagoya' while:

> thousands have died since dawn
> in the service
> of barbarous kings

represents an abrogation of public responsibility by the poet Bashō and his friends, or the heartening survival of civilised values.

One of Mahon's most complex poems on this subject is 'Rage for Order' (*Lives*, 1972), in which poetry is, at first, seen as self-indulgent:

> a dying art,
> an eddy of semantic scruple
> in an unstructurable sea

but which ends with the acknowledgement that its 'terminal ironies' may be vital to the enterprise of re-building. Nonetheless, in the poem 'In Belfast' (*Night-Crossing*, 1968), Mahon chastises himself that his

                                          desperate city
        should engage more than [his] casual interest,
        exact more interest than [his] casual pity.

There is certainly nothing 'casual' about his portrayal of his
native place in 'Ecclesiastes', a controlled explosion of a poem in
which Mahon blasts the grip evangelical religion has on Belfast.
He addresses one of the 'God-fearing, God- / chosen purist little
puritan[s]' who control the city and laments the 'dank churches,
the empty streets, / the shipyard silence, the tied-up swings' that
their self-righteous zeal has created.

    His disillusionment is echoed in 'The Last of the Fire Kings'
(*The Snow Party*), in which the speaker yearns to escape from the
'fire-loving / people' who demand that he, like them, inhabit:

            a world of
        sirens, bin-lids
        and bricked-up windows–

Contrastingly, in 'Afterlives' (*The Snow Party*), a return to Belfast
has Mahon stepping ashore:

                    in a fine rain
        to a city so changed
        by five years of war
        I scarcely recognise
        The places I grew up in

He then speculates that if he had stayed behind

        and lived it bomb by bomb,
        I might have grown up at last
        and learnt what is meant by home.

    At this point I must mention two other poets of this generation,
James Simmons and Padraic Fiacc, each of whom has produced
books dominated by the Troubles. The simplicity of the ballad

form is poignantly appropriate in 'Claudy' (*West Strand Visions*, 1974), by the songwriter and poet James Simmons, a ballad about the 1972 bombing of the County Derry village in which nine people died. Refuting the IRA's attempts to excuse the murders, it ends with the withering lines:

> Meanwhile, to Dungiven the killers have gone,
> And they're finding it hard to get through on the phone.

The devastating effect of violence on the lives of ordinary people is approached from a different perspective in Simmons' elegy 'Lament for a Dead Policeman' (*From the Irish*, 1985), two inter-related monologues spoken by the murdered man's widow and sister, and modelled on Eibhlín Dubh Ní Chonaill's magnificent eighteenth-century Gaelic elegy and love poem 'The Lament for Art Ó Laoghaire'. The elegiac note is struck even more starkly in the work of Padraic Fiacc, nicknamed by a foreign journalist 'Der Bomben Poet'. Fiacc's collection *Nights in the Bad Place* (1997) presents Belfast as an urban nightmare in which people's domestic lives are transformed into a world of 'bin-lid-shielded battle-ship-grey-faced-kids', a world of 'gelignite in the tool shed / and grenades in the scullery larder', 'of genitals roasted with a shipyard worker's blowlamp'. These poems are painfully direct in their exploration of the Troubles.

A third generation of gifted Ulster poets emerged in the 70s – most notably Paul Muldoon, Tom Paulin and Ciaran Carson – and they have each produced book-length collections permeated by an awareness of history and contemporary events in Northern Ireland. 'Lunch with Pancho Villa', the opening poem of Paul Muldoon's collection, *Mules* (1977), uses acerbic humour to explore the subject of poetic responsibility. In the poem, a freely imagined version of the Mexican revolutionary drinks 'untroubled Muscatel' and sneers at the young poet for writing rondeaux while 'People are getting themselves killed'. He advises him to 'look around', 'listen to the news' and 'get down to something true, / Something a little nearer home'. The fact that the 'stars and horses, pigs and trees', which are dismissed as subject matter by the revolutionary, figure constantly in the collection that follows suggests that Muldoon resists such reductive pressures to be, as it were, a war poet.

The theme of artistic responsibility recurs in Muldoon's poetry. In 'The Boundary Commission' (*Why Brownlee Left*, 1980), the central figure stands in a village where the border runs 'Down the middle of the street' and wonders 'which side, if any, he should be on'. Again, the sequence '7 Middagh Street', from *Meeting the British* (1987), dramatises the thoughts of a group of artists, including Louis MacNeice, Carson McCullers, W. H. Auden, Salvador Dalí and Gypsy Rose Lee (who, at one time shared that New York address), and expands into a meditation on art, politics, sex and their interconnections. Auden, for example, seeks to put art in its place by maintaining that 'history's a twisted root with art its small, translucent fruit / and never the other way round'. MacNeice, on the other hand, questions the claims made by Auden in his poem 'In Memory of W. B. Yeats', that poetry makes nothing happen and counters that it 'not only can, but must'.

Muldoon's own explorations of the Troubles are richly thought-provoking. A number of his poems focus on the attitudes and beliefs that shape lives, for better or worse, in Ireland and elsewhere. 'The Weepies' (*Why Brownlee Left*), features a gang of boys who attend the Saturday matinee at their local Hippodrome. Their leader is Will Hunter whose particular gift is that he can peel an orange 'In a single, fluent gesture'. On this occasion, expecting the usual Western, they find themselves watching a 'weepie' and are embarrassed to have their masculine securities shattered by altogether messier human realities embodied in the life of the 'lonesome drifter' and the unhappiness of the adults portrayed on the screen. The extravagant unfurling of the boys' handkerchiefs, 'Like flags of surrender', catches the fullness of their emotional awakening. The speaker is forced to acknowledge the power of emotion, to believe that 'something fell asunder / In even Will Hunter's hands'. It becomes evident as the poem progresses that the use of images of masculinity (the Pathé Rooster, the gleaming muscles of the Rank organisation's muscle-man beating his gong, Will Hunter's surname and Christian name) are all leading towards a sense of the poem as a serio-comic undermining of the 'no surrender' mentality in personal and political spheres. Not only is Will Hunter the alpha male in the gang but he is also linked to the loyalist's motto, 'No Surrender'. He is a Junior William of Orange, as it were.

Muldoon manages all this with the admirable lightness of touch that characterises both his longer poems 'The More a Man Has the More a Man Wants' and '7 Middagh Street', for example, as well as lyrics such as 'Meeting the British' and 'Aisling'. The latter is a clever re-working of the 'aisling' or 'vision' poem of Gaelic literature, in which a beautiful woman, personifying Irish nationalism, appears to the poet, yearning for deliverance from England. In Muldoon's 'Aisling' (*Quoof*, 1983), the speaker encounters a seductive woman on his way home from the pub. She promises abundance but brings also the threat of disease and the poet is forced to attend the VD clinic at the Royal Victoria Hospital in Belfast where a hunger striker who has just called off his fast is being treated. This sets one of the mythologies of romantic Irish nationalism against the harsh reality of the Troubles. On this occasion, the speaker has escaped infection and the hunger striker is in recovery, but the poem leaves us pondering the potentially deceptive and destructive nature of certain romantic ideals, both personal and public.

Muldoon's contemporary, Tom Paulin, brings a more caustic, angry note to bear on history and religion. His collection *Liberty Tree* (1985) is, on one level, a loving quest for the radical, free-thinking, Presbyterians of the late eighteenth century in Ireland, a quest he shares with John Hewitt. Many of these Presbyterians were members of the Society of the United Irishmen, committed to Catholic emancipation and parliamentary reform, and Paulin contrasts their breadth of vision with the narrowness and aridity of contemporary sectarianism. The poem 'Desertmartin', for example, is sorrowful and angry in its attack on the blighting impact of fundamentalist religions, whether in Ulster, or the Islamic dictatorships:

> Here the Word has withered to a few
> Parched certainties, and the charred stubble
> Tightens like a black belt, a crop of Bibles.

There is a thinly disguised reference to the Reverend Ian Paisley as the speaker describes seeing:

> a plain
> Presbyterian grace sour, then harden,
> As a free strenuous spirit changes
> [...] it shouts
> For the Big Man to lead his wee people
> To a clean white prison, their scorched tomorrow.

The sorrow and anger of such poems is tempered elsewhere in *Liberty Tree* by a kind of savage humour, especially in 'A Rum Cove, a Stout Cove' and 'Manichean Geography' where Paulin portrays ramshackle dead-end places, the fag end of British colonialism, or satirises cargo cults and their tawdry gods, the fractured loyalties of a culture waving a flag it 'loves and curses'. This flag appears first as a key image in the early poem 'Settlers' (*A State of Justice*, 1977), and is central to the collection *Fivemiletown* (1987). The Northern Unionists' sense of betrayal at the suspension of Stormont and the signing of the Anglo-Irish Agreement is sympathetically portrayed in poems such as 'Sure I'm a Cheat Aren't We All', 'An Ulster Unionist Walks the Streets of London' and 'The Defenestration of Hillsborough', in the last of which the speaker bluntly defines their choice – 'either to jump or get pushed'. The defenestration image is one of a number which link the experience of Northern Irish Protestants to the history of Protestant Europe, particularly during the Thirty Years' War. The collection *Fivemiletown* ends with a longer poem, 'The Caravans on Luneburg Heath' in which the main subjects are the role of writers and language in times of political upheaval. The poet, who earlier in the poem refers to his 'powerless knowledge' as he drives across Ulster, goes back to school, as it were, to be 'born again', to have his education revised, in the light of what has been explored in the poem.

In Ciaran Carson's collections *The Irish for No* (1987) and *Belfast Confetti* (1989) the menacing atmosphere of the city is caught more intensely than in the work of any other Northern Irish poet. Carson's Belfast is an elusive, labyrinthine city, the maps of which are never entirely trustworthy. It has the solidity of bricks and mortar, but it is also a construct of memory and imagination, a city that disappears and renews itself daily. One version exists in the recollections of 'The Exiles' Club' of expats who meet in the Wollongong Bar in Adelaide, Australia and have spent years reconstructing the Falls from memory (*The Irish for No*). While in 'Question Time' (*Belfast Confetti*), another Falls Road exists in the memory of a man who sets out on a bicycle to visit the streets of his childhood, is kidnapped and interrogated as an interloper and finds that his life depends on his ability to describe accurately a neighbourhood that no longer physically exists.

The Belfast depicted in these books crackles with tension. In '33333' (*The Irish for No*), for example, the speaker, taking a taxi to the Holy Land area, begins to relax, only to feel himself frighteningly disoriented, as he realises:

> I know this place like the back of my hand, except
> My hand is cut off at the wrist.

The images here are of dislocation and amputation in a place that the speaker would like to think of as familiar. He finds himself conversing with an invisible person behind a grille and arrives at 'an open door [he] never knew existed'. The traveller is not quite sure, to begin with, of his destination, but where had he arrived? And what of the sudden, shocking, unexplained image of the hand cut off at the wrist? It suggests the bloody, amputated Red Hand of Ulster and brutally undermines the ease and sense of recognition that the speaker is beginning to feel.

Throughout the collection *Belfast Confetti,* the city is portrayed as an ominous place of assignations, kneecappings and bombings, of code-named undercover operations and the confidential telephone, of advances in surveillance technology, such as the 'lazy swivelling' of the security camera and the 'Twiggy' Night Operation Device, of the omnipresent helicopter, of the bomb disposal expert on TV whose face is in shadow and the victim identified by the teeth marks left in an apple. There is not much room for optimism in this world, but neither is it relentlessly bleak. The poem 'Night Out' depicts a beleaguered kind of normality. A group of people listen to music in a pub while a gun battle rages outside:

> So, the sentence of the night
> Is punctuated through and through by rounds of drink, of bullets, of applause.

In 'The Knee' the victim of a punishment shooting takes his young son onto his undamaged knee, promising, perhaps, an alternative, though somewhat precarious future.

While these poems are ambiguous, there is a more hopeful note in the group of poems in *Belfast Confetti* which celebrate the dignity, wisdom and warm humanity of Carson's postman father. When, in 'Bedside Story', he makes bird shapes on the wall with his fingers, the images contrast with those in an earlier poem in the collection, 'Bloody Hand', in which a paramilitary, explaining how killing is 'child's play', cocks his finger at someone's head. Taken together, *The Irish for No* and *Belfast Confetti* have a substantial, cumulative impact, partly due to their shared themes, topography and imagery. Those Falls Road exiles turn up again, for example, as do particular street names and bars, and Carson is repeatedly drawn to images of urban dereliction, transient security equipment and maps of Belfast's industrial history. *Belfast Confetti* takes its title from a poem of the same name in *The Irish for No*. The phrase is used as a slang term for the screws, bolts and nails flung by rioters or used in nail bombs during the Troubles, and inventively combines images of violence with punctuation images throughout – an explosion as an asterisk, a burst of gunfire as a hyphenated line. The reference to the 'fount of broken type', the speaker's attempt to 'complete a sentence in his head' and the riotous punctuation suggest also the constrictions and limitations of writing about the Troubles. The concluding line: 'Where am I coming from? Where am I going? A fusillade of question marks' combines the menacing presence of an interrogator with an image of the writer trying urgently to restore a threatened identity, to re-establish a solid sense of location in the midst of chaos.

Much more obliquely preoccupied with the Troubles and the interaction of the Irish past and present is the poetry of Medbh

McGuckian, most particularly in *Captain Lavender* (1994), which takes as its epigraph a statement by Picasso in 1944: '*I have not painted the war...but I have no doubt that the war is in...these paintings I have done.*' In *Drawing Ballerinas* (2001) the title poem is an elegy commemorating Ann Frances Owens, a schoolfellow and neighbour of the poet, who was killed in the Abercorn Café explosion in 1972. Book title and poem take their cue from Matisse's response to a question about how he had survived the war artistically; he replied that he had spent the war years 'drawing ballerinas'.

McGuckian's poems have a mysterious quality and a kind of privacy, both in her love poems and Troubles poems. Verbs of looking and seeing and not seeing provide the dominant images in 'The Dead are More Alive' (*Drawing Ballerinas*), as the speaker explores the complications of response to violence and images of violence. McGuckian is reported to have said that the poem was written in response to the murder of two army corporals in West Belfast. The men's abduction and beating were captured live on television, though the murders were not, but the sheer barbarism of the event is captured in the lines:

> Even if you did not see it, nevertheless
> it grazed the skin of your mind
> with a slashing as if on flesh
> by an open knife blade, slicing
> everything in two.

Elsewhere in the poem McGuckian reflects on the impact of seeing such gruesome images and concludes that:

> You were shielded against what you saw
> only by never looking away,
> you broke down what you saw
> by not turning your head,

suggesting that by observing events it is somehow possible to remain at a distance from them.

No sooner had Carson, Muldoon and company begun to make their mark, than yet another group of Ulster poets appeared, establishing a kind of continuity that stretched back to the 1940s. Alan Gillis is the most strongly urban of these. His Belfast is a bleak, menacing place, destabilised by alcohol and drugs, and perpetually on the edge of violence. The macabre poem, '12 October, 1994' (*Somebody, Somewhere*, 2004), presents a gallery of paramilitary hard men such as Victor 'Steel-Plate' Hogg, Benny 'Vindaloo' McVeigh and Frankie 'Ten-pints' Fraser, the latter of whom is overheard pronouncing on their collective and individual futures – 'No Victor, nobody's going to fucking disband'. The uncertain, transitional feel of post-Troubles Northern Ireland is evident in Gillis' 'Lagan Weir' (*Hawks and Doves*, 2007). The circular structure of the poem gives us a sense that the speaker feels trapped and the fact that he is standing on a bridge suggests that he has reached a pivotal moment. He is 'in two minds', caught between 'a dove in one ear saying / look the other way, [and] a hawk in the other / braying self-righteous fury'. There is an ominous sense that:

> things are going to get
> a whole lot worse before they get better.

but, throughout the poem, a flock of starlings – bright and energetic – provides a contrast to the lack of direction below. They remind us that we

> might as well take a leap and try following
> after that scatter-wheeling circus of shadows
> as they slowly turn and make their dark way
> homeward, never slowing, not knowing
> the way things are going.

Leontia Flynn's vision of the 'new' Belfast is to be found in her poems 'Leaving Belfast', 'Belfast', 'Letter to Friends' and 'The Peace Lily'. 'Leaving Belfast', from *Drives* (2008), is addressed to the one leaving and builds up a picture of a city where:

for every torn-up billboard [...]
there's some scrap of hope in the young, in the good looks
of women,
in the leafiness of the smart zones, in the aerobatics of
starlings.

It is a city that will 'bury its past', a city that will 'paper over the
cracks / with car parks and luxury flats, it will make itself new'.
In another poem, titled 'Belfast' (*Drives*), Flynn states confidently,
'Belfast is finished and Belfast is under construction'. This line
introduces a set of images of Belfast entering a new dynamic
phase that includes 'concerts and walking tours' and 'A tourist
pamphlet [that] contains an artist's impression // of arcades,
mock-colonnades, church-spires and tapas bars'.

Flynn's 'Letter to Friends' (*Profit and Loss*, 2011), strikes a more
expansive, chatty note on the general state of the city. She cites
'a building boom and shopping malls thrown up like flotsam by
our new security'. Shopping is said to be 'done less for recreation
/ [...] /than from a kind of civic obligation'. Despite the city's retail
therapy, the citizens are 'frequently diagnosed as depressed, tired
or infertile'. Flynn strikes a note of wary optimism about the future
in her poem 'The Peace Lily'. The flower experiences 'calm neglect'
but endures modestly in a corner of the room.

The note here is similar to that struck by Sinéad Morrissey in
her poem 'Tourism', from *Between Here and There* (2002), which
satirises peace-dividend Belfast's growing popularity as a tourist
destination. The poem is a kind of guided tour of the city in which
its Troubles landmarks are shamelessly exploited:

We take them to those streets
They want to see most, at first,

as though it's all over and safe behind bus glass

Even though the speaker tells us 'Our day has come', the phrase 'as
though it's all over' implies that the peace is not entirely secure.
However, the city has an 'off-beat, headstrong, suicidal charm' and
visitors are invited to 'keep coming here [...] Diffuse the gene pool,

confuse the local kings, // infect us with your radical ideas'. The poem 'In Belfast', from *Between Here and There*, depicts the city as inhaling and exhaling money. Returning after ten years' absence, Morrissey tells herself that Belfast is as 'real' as anywhere she has lived, 'More real, even, with this history's dent and fracture // splitting the atmosphere'. The future is left 'unspoken', the past 'unencountered and unaccounted for' and the place so intimately elusive that the speaker declares herself 'as much at home here as I will ever be'.

The poetry of the Troubles emanates from all parts of Ulster, but mostly from the two main cities. Colette Bryce's autobiographical ballad 'Derry', from *The Whole and Rain-domed Universe* (2014), begins in imitation of Louis MacNeice's 'Carrickfergus' – 'I was born between the Creggan and the Bogside' echoes 'I was born in Belfast between the mountain and the gantries'. She goes on confidently, and with her tongue planted firmly in her cheek, to paint a lively and compelling picture of growing up in Derry:

> The adult world had tumbled into hell
>
> from where it wouldn't find its way
> for thirty years. The local priest
> played Elvis tunes and made us pray
> for starving children, and for peace.

Bryce makes effective use of detail to trace the course of the Troubles: the hunger strikes, the strip searching of women in Armagh prison, Gerry Adams' mouth out of sync on the TV news, unemployment, emigration to England, tensions domestic and public. The famous Derry sardonic humour is given its place:

> The proof that Jesus was a Derry man?
> Thirty-three, unemployed and living with his mother,
> the old joke ran.

The poem ends with the poet flying out of Derry and seeing the place 'grow small' before her eyes until she cannot 'see it clearly any more'.

In other poems such as 'The Republicans' and 'The Brits', both from *The Whole and Rain-domed Universe*, and 'When I Land in Northern Ireland', from *Self-Portrait in the Dark* (2008), Bryce displays a lightness of touch even when catching the tensions within her home city. For example, in 'The Brits', she recalls an unexpected moment of humanity when a group of soldiers raided her childhood home and, like the 'gormless young fellas' they actually were, did as her mother told them and left their guns 'stacked, clackety-clack' downstairs with their leader so as not to frighten the 'children in their beds'. Years later she dreams of the soldiers as tiny action figures and says she would like to

> remove their camouflage and radios,
> to dress them up in doll-sized clothes, little high-street shirts,
> jeans, trainers, the strip of ordinary sons and brothers.
> I'd like to hand them back to their mothers.

Irony is also the chosen mode in 'And They Call It Lovely Derry', from *The Full Indian Rope Trick* (2005), in which a group of Catholic and Protestant children from Derry/Londonderry are sent to Florida to 'mix for three weeks in a normal society'. However, while there the speaker finds that Florida has its own form of sectarianism when her host turns out to be a racist and it is no surprise when the concert they give on the final night founders on old divisions:

> We harmonised on all the songs
> but fell apart with the grande finale,
> the well-rehearsed 'O I know a wee spot ...'
> as the group split between London and Lovely.

It is clear that their experience has not had the desired effect and that, once home, they will slip back into the sectarian groove which is in fact 'normal' to them.

Another poem about the effect of the Troubles on a child has the following epigraph:

On the morning of March 6, 1984, Mr William McConnell, assistant governor of the Maze Prison, was outside his home, checking underneath his car for explosive devices, when he was shot dead in front of his wife and three-year-old daughter.

The main speaker in the book-length poem *The Sun is Open* (2021) is the poet Gail McConnell, the three-year-old girl who witnessed the murder. The poem begins with an imagined kiss of life and becomes a search for an elusive father. The search is conducted partly through the contents of what McConnell refers to as the 'DAD BOX', a mixture of personal and official documents relating to her father's life and death. The background to the central event is violence on the streets, the voices of unidentified people, a family's struggle to come to grips with the horror of their experience and the innocent childhood world of toys, sweets and cartoons. As befits the content, the structure is fragmentary, a gathering of images and insights. Ciaran Carson has compared the box-like verses to inches of newsprint and the entries in an account book. An earlier poem by McConnell, titled 'Type Face', was a shocked response, not only to her father's death, but to the way it was recorded in official documents and reports, such as that of the Historical Enquiries Team. *The Sun is Open* is more measured, if one may use such a term. Heaney's comment that poets must seek images 'adequate to [their] predicament' comes to mind more forcefully in relation to McConnell than to any other Ulster poet because her 'predicament' is so much more immediate and personal:

> What a paper trail this was what
> does it all add up to lead to not
> a murder book and
> not an archive not a fever not a
> feeling of all these things and none
> it's what dislodges in my body
> when I hear balloons pop pop

Revisiting *A Rage for Order*, its variety of themes and multitude of voices has proved salutary and affirmative. It mourns the destruction and loss of life caused by 30 years of violence and celebrates the survival of the individual. It elevates what is normal, preserves what is humane and teaches us to be compassionate and tolerant. More importantly, as we continue on our journey towards reconciliation, it will undoubtedly play an ongoing part in the exploration of our Troubles heritage.

I'd like to end with one of the most striking post-ceasefire poems, 'Progress' by Alan Gillis (*Somebody, Somewhere* 2004), a forlorn, ironic fantasy in which the Troubles are thrown into reverse. It may be read on a number of levels; on the surface it seems to flirt with the possibility of rewriting history and resurrecting the dead but, on another level, it serves as a bitter reminder that we can't escape the past.

Progress

They say that for years Belfast was backwards
and it's great now to see some progress.
So I guess we can look forward to taking boxes
from the earth. I guess that ambulances
will leave the dying back amidst the rubble
to be explosively healed. Given time,
one hundred thousand particles of glass
will create impossible patterns in the air
before coalescing into the clarity
of a window. Through which, a reassembled head
will look out and admire the shy young man
taking his bomb from the building and driving home.

Based on a lecture given at Trinity College Dublin on 11 November 2021.

'The World Unmade': Frank Ormsby in Conversation

This conversation between Frank Ormsby and Lucy Collins took place online on 24 January 2023 and was revised and expanded for publication here. It presents six recent poems by Ormsby – all of which will appear in his next collection, The Tumbling Paddy – *and situates these in the context of his wider achievements as a poet and editor.*

The Tumbling Paddy

No jiggery pokery.
It cuts up rough, moves
like a clumsy clockwork,
the hobbledehoy
of farmyard machinery.
In its blunderings after lumpy clay
it is gobbledygook in motion,
a hop-along hauled by a tractor.
It never misses
an angle, hirpling as though half-crippled,
perfecting the work of the harrow.
It completes also its own ungainly rhythms,
the stumble-bum routines
of limp-along Paddy.

Nothing extravagant, no skip and jump, just
a job-well done,
the field settling behind.
The tumbler-done-tumbling,
it will lie in the barn for three seasons,
its tatterdemalion cover gathering rust.

You've chosen 'The Tumbling Paddy' as the title poem of your new collection. Can you tell us a little about the inspiration for the poem, and how it expresses some of the wider concerns in your new book?

Well, a tumbling paddy was a piece of farmyard machinery, a kind of giant rake, originally pulled by a horse, and later by a tractor and used to turn and gather hay a few days after it had been cut. It would be very interesting to know the origin of the name – it certainly suggests that it was invented or popularised in Ireland. Seeing it reminded me somehow of a rough country dance, full of awkward energetic movements, and I thought too of Seamus Heaney's poem 'The Settle Bed' in which he deliberately chooses unwieldy language to convey the roughness of the wood. I think I'm doing something similar in this poem in the way I make deliberate use of clumsy terms such as 'hobbledehoy', 'hirpling' and 'tatterdemalion'. I feel slightly fraudulent about choosing this as the title of the book because, if you really get down to it, it's not that representative of the poems, which cover a range of subjects such as animals, local history, memory and loss. However, I found that once I had the phrase 'the tumbling paddy' in my head, I couldn't let go of it – or rather, it wouldn't let go of me.

Why do you think you find yourself returning to rural landscapes at this stage in your writing life?

Although I have written extensively about life in the city, to some extent, I never really left the rural landscape behind. In each of my previous books there have been poems about the people, places and objects of my childhood in County Fermanagh. The material of childhood is never quite exhausted. Indeed, it's natural that as you grow older you look back on the past through different eyes; with a level of maturity and understanding that you didn't have before. When you get to my age images return to you with a resonance they lacked at the time and, if you are lucky, these cycles of return and renewal can bless you with a late flowering, a fresh perspective, a certain sturdy resilience in the face of illness. Over the last three or four collections I've been going back to my uncle's farm – a little farm of just sixteen acres. We practically lived there and took part in all the farming activities. Everybody was involved. My mother, for example, was an expert at building hayricks. In fact, I wrote a precursor to 'The Tumbling Paddy' called 'The Builder' in which the main image is of her standing in the middle of the rick and having the hay fed up to her on pitchforks so that she could flatten it out. I remember watching with admiration as she shaped and formed the towering rick while exchanging greetings with passersby who called and waved from bus windows.

That's such a wonderful image of community – how do you go about capturing this energy in your poems? Does it have an impact on the forms you choose?

That's an interesting way of reading that image. I've always thought of my mother as quite a solitary figure, immersed in the daily struggle while life went on around her, but in fact my poems are populated by whole communities of isolated people. More recently, I have tended to write sequences of poems that focus on particular groups and generate their own cumulative energy. For example, the farming folk of 'The Rain Barrel', families awaiting news of 'The Disappeared' and the artistic community of Irish Impressionists in 'Twenty-six Irish Paintings'.

As for matters of form, the form of a poem is usually prompted by a line or an image, rather than being a deliberate choice. Most of my poems could be classed as free verse, but with certain internal patterns of repetition or half-rhyme which grow naturally and randomly out of the poems. Having said that, I have a soft spot for the dramatic monologue. My collection, *A Northern Spring*, contains a sequence of about 30 poems about the GIs in the north of Ireland preparing for the Normandy landings. Very often these are dramatic monologues in which the American soldiers are allowed to speak – or I imagine how they would speak – about their experiences in Ireland, France and after their return to the United States.

Your own engagement with other voices and experiences has also created some powerful poems. 'Apples, Normandy, 1944' engages with the difficult relationship between art and war. And you once said in an interview that it was a poem that felt as though it had been written by someone else. Is that a liberating thing?

Yes, I think you would want to have this experience with every poem you sit down to write. There are some poems which you have to work on, and others that come out almost fully formed and there's nothing you can do to make them any better – without necessarily thinking that they're wonderful poems. 'Apples, Normandy, 1944' is certainly one of those. After it was published in *The Observer*, I got a couple of letters asking if I had had a particular war artist in mind. That was very pleasing because, although the artist in the poem is an invented figure, the poem had obviously touched something in readers and connected with them imaginatively. It concerned the idea that a war artist might get fed up with his official function and want instead to follow his own creative direction, which in the poem is painting apples. In a larger sense this is about the pressure of artistic expectations and therefore relates to Ulster poets as they started writing about the Troubles.

Did you feel those expectations very strongly yourself?

Only as a kind of irritant at first but, as time passed, the idea that we were expected to write poems about the Troubles became a significant concern. All the Ulster writers and poets were infected by that, and the issue was to the fore or in the background of a lot of poems from the North during those years. My anthology, *A Rage for Order: Poems of the Northern Ireland Troubles*, was in part an attempt to define how central the Troubles had become as a theme.

A number of your poems focus closely on the world of everyday objects and small-scale things. Why is there such an emphasis on attention to detail in your work, do you think?

On one level it stops you being pompous. My most recent books are full of images of everyday objects such as tin buckets, rain barrels and scarecrows and these keep you rooted in the fabric of ordinary life. However, even from my first book, *A Store of Candles,* I seem to have had this preoccupation with the minutiae of day-to-day existence. There's a section there which looks at the small ads that you find in newspapers: 'The small ads give notice of a world / Where little is wasted'. The emphasis here is on how items that appear insignificant actually have an inherent value.

In a more recent book, *The Rain Barrel,* there's a poem called 'Small Things' about a trip to Belfast's Waterworks Park in search of a heron which had taken up residence there. I had recently come out of hospital and my daily walk around the park had become a small, comforting ritual during which I frequently crossed paths with a group of men I imagined were doing something similar, However, the heron was nowhere to be seen that day and the old boys obviously wanted to make up for the fact that I'd missed it, so they directed me to keep an eye out for the egrets instead. When life is fragile it's the small things that bring us pleasure: 'the old boys / in their baseball caps delighting in small things, / the small things made precious by their delight.' I suppose my delight in small things is also evident in my use of the haiku which is both compact and expansive. In the sequence 'Small World' from *Fireflies* I think the form allows me to reflect the extraordinary qualities of the ordinary:

> Sensing a haiku
> opportunity – those two
> blackbirds, right on cue.

There's an interesting range of birds and animals in your poetry – from agricultural animals to wild or exotic creatures – and these seem to be growing in imaginative importance for you. Can you say more about why you gravitate towards animal life?

I think I'm conscious of the otherness of animals, and this is a stimulating, liberating experience. Many of the creatures that have found their way into my latest poems are not native to Ireland or have been encountered in another environment: racoons, cicadas, the rhinoceros, all appear in stylised forms in the new book. Animals feature in my earlier work too but even the cow sequence in *The Rain Barrel* registers that sense of difference – 'We never got used to cows, / the oddness of the odd / inhabiting our fields'. However, I don't devote much creative energy to thinking deeply about my own relationship with the animal world; it's the imaginative response that's the important thing.

Racoon

My favourite among the lone foragers,
he comes up out of the woods at dusk
as though he has had an invitation to dinner.
We retreat indoors and he goes head to head
with our trash cans, mounting the first
in what looks like rough foreplay,
then shouldering and up-ending and rifling
with a verve that sounds half-glee, half-hunger.
Avoiding a full-frontal with that muscular snout
we lock ourselves in the kitchen. He is dressed
for autumn in his mask and the grey-brown banded jumper
that almost makes him invisible.
Indifferent to our attentions
he makes off at last, a snuffling Algonquin, carrying
whatever his spree has yielded. He grumbles as he runs,
would not, even if he understood such matters,
forgive the world its unshared plenty.

One of the things that strikes me most in re-reading your work is how funny many of the poems are. Even recent work that deals with quite dark themes, such as your experience of Parkinson's Disease. Do you feel that humour is essential when confronting difficult subjects?

I've always had quite a dark and irreverent sense of humour. There are examples of this throughout my work, but the first that springs to mind is one of the Normandy poems which manages to deal with both the savagery of war and racism:

I Stepped On A Small Landmine

I stepped on a small landmine in the *bocage*
and was spread, with three others, over a field
of burnt lucerne.
The bits they shipped to Georgia at the request
of my two sisters were not entirely me.
If dead men laughed, I would have laughed the day
the committee for dead heroes honoured me,
and honoured too the mangled testicles
of Leroy Earl Johnson.

More recently, the humour in my Parkinson's sequence is a mixture of flippancy and defiance. There are undercurrents of anger and frustration but undoubtedly the process of writing these poems helped me to a sense of perspective, wry equanimity and the discovery that it's possible to get some enjoyment from uncomfortable truths. I have written about both the symptoms of Parkinson's, for instance the tremors and loss of my 'teacherly gulder', and the – sometimes worse – side effects of the medication such as hallucinations. This theme is continued in the new collection in the poem 'I appear to have mislaid'.

I appear to have mislaid

I've got more to lose than I thought:
room-key, passport, pocket diary,

wallet, debit card, mobile phone,
the piece of paper on which I have written
my National Insurance number,
the piece of paper on which I have written
the first line of a poem, and the title
of a book I'm thinking of buying,
the pieces of paper on which I have recorded
my hotel registration details, my luggage ticket,
and the boarding pass for my flight home,
my reading glasses, the tablet to be taken
mid-afternoon, my insulin pen, my security badge,
miscellaneous receipts and expenses,
a piece of paper with your telephone number and address,
a recent photo of you. Jesus, I'm tired. I would go to bed now,
were it not that I appear to have mislaid
the key to my suitcase. My pyjamas are in there,
I am almost certain.
I have more to lose than I thought.
I have everything to lose.

It's interesting that this poem is full of missing pieces of paper with numbers, addresses, lines of poetry and book titles. A number of your recent poems reflect directly on the written word in this way. Can you tell us a little about your process of writing – do you return to earlier notes and drafts, or rely on new inspiration each time?

As I said earlier, there are some poems that come out almost fully formed, but there are others that I have struggled with, and still more that eventually spring from a single line or image that I have stored away. If the process of writing becomes too laborious you can end up with a poem that is essentially inert, and that's tough going for the poet, as well as the reader, so sometimes it is better to leave a poem and come back to it. In some cases, I might have set a poem aside for years and then suddenly I think of a way I might complete it. This return to unfinished poems is an important thing for me. I edited John Hewitt's *Collected Poems* and learned a lot by going through his papers and manuscript poems. When Hewitt returned to Belfast in the early 1970s, he set about finishing unfinished poems from the 1940s that he'd kept in his notebooks for decades. Similarly, I wrote a sequence of poems about a part of New York State that I used to visit, Westchester County, but many of the drafts remained unfinished and I found myself coming back to them a year later, two years later, in some cases three years later. This is also true of some of the poems in *The Tumbling Paddy*, and I'm hoping by returning to the poems now I'll be able to bring them to their final state.

How much attention do you pay to the relationship between poems in a collection, or to the links between different aspects of your work?

Of course, there are very obvious links between the poems in the various sequences within my later books, but there are other ways in which single poems scattered throughout a collection can build upon each other thematically and stylistically. One of the most satisfying aspects of putting a book together is the linking or positioning of the poems, and in my most recent book, *The Rain Barrel*, there are about a dozen poems on the subject of the Disappeared. The search for these victims of the Troubles, who were abducted, murdered and secretly buried in isolated boglands and beaches almost half a century ago, has been ongoing for many years and in the same way that they periodically enter the public consciousness I deliberately chose to disperse the poems throughout the book so that, like the Disappeared themselves, they sporadically rise to the surface.

In terms of my work as an anthologist, the selecting of poems is, in itself, an aesthetic exercise and the grouping of poems within an anthology is just as important is it is within an original collection. In addition, the process of putting together an anthology involves thinking about poetry all the time, and it inevitably challenges your own sense of what makes a successful poem. It is sometimes clear to see how a poem I am considering for selection could have been improved with some radical self-editing and this has certainly had a lasting impact on my approach to editing my own work. As a teacher I have often advised students to identify their most cherished image and then be prepared to discard it entirely. By this I mean that I am all too aware that a poem can be weakened by the poet's determination to include a particular line or image. This is a tendency we all have to guard against, and I am much more likely now to cut poems radically than before.

Recently I found myself revisiting and applying this process to a sequence of poems that I wrote a few years ago called 'The Terrace'.

The Terrace

Now that the terrace of workers' houses
called Wharf Road has been reconstructed
– each house painted in a different colour –
and the pavements have been re-laid, it is time to hand the
    keys
to the young professionals. They are giddy with expectation
and already a kind of community. Soon there will be
a neighbourhood watch and a development committee.
They will look up – how many times a day? – as the world
    flies in and out.
They will support the new supermarket
and greet the arrival of Caffè Nero.
They will object to the airport's plans for a new runway.
Month by month they will establish their lives around
    Starbucks,
or Subway, or Costa,
will claim the city as a maritime nook
of café society. Just now it is the season
of the hanging basket and the night-shift
of automatic porch-lights. Across the river
the homeless settle on park benches, out of sight,
and the skies darken there with a different history.

The Terrace in Winter

Sleet arrives at the window
with an urge to be snow.
It fills the sky with ambition.
But the sea swallows fall after fall.

Wharfs, piers, quays develop a wintry interim,
the sleet bidding to shape the next snowflake.
The wettest melt where they land,
Fade back into the world indivisible, the world unmade.

A lot of your recent work engages with change, often in an elegiac mode – I'm thinking, in particular, of the sequence 'Autumn Burial' and the formal variety in its approach to death and memorialisation. Have you always been an elegist, or has this aspect of your work intensified?

Well, I used to get quite annoyed when reviewers focused exclusively on my elegiac poems to the detriment of those that are more light-hearted. It seems to me, if you're not responding to the funny parts, you're not reading the poems at all. A few years ago, I wrote a humorous poem that is a kind of elegy for myself. It's called 'The Hour-Glass' and is the final poem in my collection, *Goat's Milk*. It imagines how my wife might dispose of my ashes and suggests that she should put me to work by '[sifting] a handful or two with care / into the top-half of an hour-glass / and set me to pass the days on our bedside table'.

On a more serious note, aspects of elegy have certainly been evident in my poems from early on. There are poems about my father in all my books. He died when I was about twelve years old, and I think these are attempts to recover his presence or to come to grips with my sense of him. The opportunity is in fact fairly limited because not only did he die when I was very young but, for some time before his death, he had suffered a number of strokes and his speech was impaired, so our points of contact were few. My poems 'In Memoriam' from *A Store of Candles*, and 'The Gap on my Shelf', from *The Ghost Train*, capture this loss. I think many share this feeling: that the people you wanted to sit down and have a conversation with either had the reticence of country people or – in this case – had lost their speech and were difficult to understand. I never had the impression that my father was saying anything radically important when he was alive but now I can think of all the questions I would have liked to have asked him and that feeds into the poems. There is a sense of regret, of having missed out on all kinds of things – a lack of communication that can no longer be put right.

I think the sequence of elegies in *The Tumbling Paddy* has more of my voice in it than some of the other poems. It's a combination of elegies for my mother, who died many years ago, and for my first wife, who died last October. Originally, I chose 'Hurricane Ophelia' as the title but then I thought this would be misleading, and the Shakespearean reference might send readers down the wrong path completely, so I decided on 'Autumn Burials'. I'd like to finish by reading from this sequence.

Autumn Burials

1. Someone is making your final bed

Someone is making your final bed
out of coffin liner, a soft surround
that will leave your brow uncovered.
He aims for repose and comfort and a sense
that all these no longer matter,
except as the practical tenderness
we need to survive loss.
Someone is preparing your final face
to look up for the last time
into light from the window.

2. Laid Out for Burial

Laid out for burial you embody
then disembody your eighty-three years.
Nothing more to be said of you

that is not in the past tense.
What is said will keep open for a time
the memories through which you will be forgotten.

3. Finalities

Nothing so final as that leaning in
of children and grandchildren,
their lips touching your face,
their hands on yours.

Unless it be the stepping back to become
onlookers. Now the undertaker's hands
are tactfully matter-of-fact. They pat your hair
that the shroud may close over.

Then the lid, fitting exactly.
Your name on the lid.

4. No Last Words

There will be no last words to take us back
to where it started, or where it started to go wrong.
No sudden insights, no wording to clarify or mend the
brokenness. No death-bed secrets. Nothing will get said
that would light a single corner of our lives. The lost years
and their sadness are gathering in wind and rain.

5. In the Wind

Prayers in the wind, wind in the open grave,
the fits and starts of Hurricane Ophelia.
I gather the notes I have made for a poem,
like crumpled blossoms retrieved from a coffin lid,
while the big, intimate, unruly storm
hijacks my eulogy and the parson's words.

6. During Hurricane Ophelia

The worst weather in Ireland
since the Great Storm
is heading this way.

Laid out in the backroom
of the funeral parlour
you are a petite version of yourself.

I kiss the stone forehead
I have not seen
for more than twenty years.

The skies are a grey swirl
from the west. The undertaker
tucks you in.

Blessed be the cleric who jokes with an ear
to the storm: 'For all we know,
today is the end of the world.'

Between two gravestones
the gravediggers
have made your bed.

7. Elegiac

We are tuned to a seasonal longing, a slow march
of arrivals geared for departure.
There's a downbeat whisper in the blood
that is missing the ocean.

Biographical Note

Frank Ormsby was born in 1947 in Enniskillen and educated at Queen's University, Belfast. He was head of English at the Royal Belfast Academical Institution from 1976 until 2010. As editor of *The Honest Ulsterman* magazine for 20 years, and of a number of influential anthologies, such as *Poets from the North of Ireland* (1979) and *A Rage for Order: Poetry of the Northern Ireland Troubles* (1992), he was a central figure in the burgeoning of Ulster poetry since the 1960s. In 1991, he edited *The Collected Poems of John Hewitt* and, in 2007, with Michael Longley, Hewitt's *Selected Poems*. He has published seven collections of poems: *A Store of Candles* (1977) and *A Northern Spring* (1986), both of which were Poetry Book Society Choices, followed by *The Ghost Train* (1995), *Fireflies* (2009), *Goat's Milk: New and Selected Poems* (2015), *The Darkness of Snow* (2017) and *The Rain Barrel* (2019). He edited *The Blackbird's Nest: An Anthology of Poetry from Queen's University Belfast* in 2006 and subsequently was editor, with Leontia Flynn, of the Queen's poetry magazine *The Yellow Nib*. He was the Ireland Professor of Poetry from 2019–2022.

Acknowledgments

The author and publisher gratefully acknowledge the following for permission to reprint copyright material. Every effort has been made to seek copyright clearance on referenced text. If there are any omissions, UCD Press will be pleased to insert the appropriate acknowledgement in any subsequent printing or editions.

John Montague: extract from 'Falls Funeral' from *A Slow Dance* (Gallery Press, 1975). Reproduced by kind permission of the Estate of John Montague and The Gallery Press.

Seamus Heaney: extracts from 'The Other Side' and 'Funeral Rights' from *Door into the Dark* (Faber and Faber, 1969) and 'Letter to an Editor', © the Estate of Seamus Heaney. Reprinted by kind permission of the Estate of Seamus Heaney and Faber and Faber Ltd.

Michael Longley: extracts from 'Wounds', 'The Ice-Cream Man', 'Peace' and 'Ceasefire' from *Collected Poems* (Jonathan Cape, 2007), © Michael Longley 2007. Reprinted by kind permission of Penguin Books Ltd.

Derek Mahon: extracts from 'The Snow Party', 'The Last of the Fire Kings' and 'Afterlives' from *The Snow Party* (Gallery Press, 1975), 'Rage for Order' and 'Ecclesiastes' from *Lives* (Gallery Press, 1972) and 'In Belfast' from *Night Crossing* (Gallery Press, 1968). Reproduced by kind permission of the Estate of Derek Mahon and The Gallery Press.

Gail McConnell: extract from *The Sun is Open* (Penned in the Margins, 2021). Reproduced by kind permission of the author and Penned in the Margins.

Bibliography

Colette Bryce, *The Full Indian Rope Trick* (Picador, 2005).
Colette Bryce, *Self-Portrait in the Dark* (Picador, 2008).
Colette Bryce, *The Whole and Rain-domed Universe* (Picador, 2014).
Ciaran Carson, *Belfast Confetti* (Gallery Press, 1989).
Ciaran Carson, *The Irish for No* (Gallery Press, 1987).
Padraic Fiacc, *Nights in the Bad Place* (Blackstaff Press, 1977).
Padraic Fiacc, *The Wearing of the Black* (Blackstaff Press, 1974).
Leontia Flynn, *Drives* (Jonathan Cape, 2008).
Leontia Flynn, *Profit and Loss* (Jonathan Cape, 2011).
Alan Gillis, *Hawks and Doves* (Gallery Press, 2007).
Alan Gillis, *Somebody, Somewhere* (Gallery Press, 2004).
P. V. Glob, *The Bog People: Iron-Age Man Preserved*, trans. by Rupert
    Bruce-Mitford (Faber and Faber, 1969).
Seamus Heaney, *Door into the Dark* (Faber and Faber, 1969).
Seamus Heaney, *North* (Faber and Faber, 1976).
Seamus Heaney, *Seeing Things* (Faber and Faber, 1991).
John Hewitt, *Collected Poems*, ed. by Frank Ormsby (Blackstaff
    Press, 1991).
John Hewitt, *Collected Poems 1932–1967* (MacGibbon and Kee,
    1968).
John Hewitt, *Freehold and Other Poems* (Blackstaff Press, 1986).
John Hewitt, *No Rebel Word* (Frederick Muller, 1948).
John Hewitt, *Out of My Time: Poems 1967–1974* (Blackstaff Press,
    1974).
John Hewitt, *An Ulster Reckoning* (privately printed, 1971).
Michael Longley, *The Echo Gate* (Secker and Warburg, 1979).
Michael Longley, *An Exploded View* (Victor Gollancz, 1973).
Michael Longley, *The Ghost Orchid* (Jonathan Cape, 1995).
Michael Longley, *Gorse Fires* (Secker and Warburg, 1991).
Michael Longley, *No Continuing City* (Macmillan, 1969).
Gail McConnell, *The Sun is Open* (Penned in the Margins, 2021).
Medbh McGuckian, *Captain Lavender* (Gallery Press, 1994).
Medbh McGuckian, *Drawing Ballerinas* (Gallery Press, 2001).
Louis MacNeice, *Autumn Journal* (Faber and Faber, 1939).

Louis MacNeice's *Collected Poems*, ed. by E. R. Dodds (Faber and Faber, 1966).

Derek Mahon, *Lives* (Oxford University Press, 1972).

Derek Mahon, *The Snow Party* (Oxford University Press, 1975).

John Montague, *The Rough Field* (Dolmen Press, 1972).

John Montague, *A Slow Dance* (Wake Forest University Press, 1975).

Sinéad Morrissey, *Between Here and There* (Carcanet, 2002).

Paul Muldoon, *Meeting the British* (Faber and Faber, 1987).

Paul Muldoon, *Mules* (Faber and Faber, 1977).

Paul Muldoon, *Quoof* (Faber and Faber, 1983).

Paul Muldoon, *Why Brownlee Left* (Faber and Faber, 1980).

Frank Ormsby, *Fireflies* (Oxford University Press, 2009).

Frank Ormsby, *The Ghost Train* (Gallery Press, 1995).

Frank Ormsby, *Goat's Milk: New and Selected Poems* (Bloodaxe, 2015).

Frank Ormsby, *A Northern Spring* (Gallery Press, 1986).

Frank Ormsby, *A Rage for Order: Poems of the Northern Ireland Troubles* (Blackstaff Press, 1992).

Frank Ormsby, *The Rain Barrel* (Bloodaxe, 2019).

Frank Ormsby, *A Store of Candles* (Gallery Press, 1977).

Tom Paulin, *Fivemiletown* (Faber and Faber, 1987).

Tom Paulin, *Liberty Tree* (Faber and Faber, 1985).

Tom Paulin, *A State of Justice* (Faber and Faber, 1977).

Carol Rumens, *A Strange Girl in Bright Colours* (Quartet Books, 1973).

James Simmons, *From the Irish* (Blackstaff Press, 1985).

James Simmons, *Late but in Earnest* (Bodley Head, 1967).

James Simmons, *West Strand Visions* (Blackstaff Press, 1974).